How to be Happy Alone

A single's guide to a satisfying life

By

Katharine Benelli Coggeshall

Published Internationally by Spirit Kat Press

© 2017 Katharine Benelli Coggeshall

ISBN-10: 1521928770

ISBN-13: 978-1521928776

This book is dedicated to my mother, Karen.

She taught me the value of savoring every moment in life.

Table of Contents

Table of Contents

Single is a Choice

The Road That Led You Here

There are many roads leading to the well-inhabited "single town"—some are long and winding, others are short and abrupt—despite the type of road you've traveled to get here, you made it.

You are whole, and this is just the beginning of a beautiful chapter in your life.

But before you can appreciate the wonders of single town, you need to glance back and acknowledge that road for a moment. Ask yourself a few questions.

Who has traveled with you along your road? How rocky was the path? Were there detours worth repeating or avoiding in the future? Reflect passively and without judgement.

Your road is unique and says a great deal about you, what you accept, what you've been through, what you want, and perhaps what you won't tolerate. Understand your road, accept it.

In so many ways, your road is a reflection of your growth. And most growth comes with at least a bit of pain, if not a lot.

You cannot go back and change a path you've already taken, well-worn and imprinted into the earth. But your acknowledgment, understanding, and acceptance of your road can help you determine your path forward. It is **that** road which you can choose. Use the lessons you've learned to help guide you forward.

You can become a better version of yourself, reinvent yourself, because your future has yet to be determined.

Once you have acknowledged your past and accepted your reality, move forward once more and join the rest of us in single town.

Single is a Choice

Single for Now or Forever

It is rare that someone travels their life road without stopping in single town at least once. The end of a relationship or marriage is unfortunately a common occurrence. But whether you choose to remain single for a short time, a long time, or forever is up to you.

There is no right or wrong decision, only your decision.

Your previous relationship may have left you wounded. Embrace this healing time alone; there is no need to rush your decision. On the other hand, you may be eager to exit single town sooner than others recommend. This is fine too. Only you know when it's right to say good-bye to single town.

Perspective is everything when it comes to happiness, so remember that residency in single town is your choice. This is especially important when you are experiencing feelings of loneliness or doubt about your current situation. There is purpose in your time as a single and opportunity for self-growth and exploration.

If you view single town as some kind of purgatory between relationships, waiting impatiently for "real life" to begin again, you will miss out on a valuable segment of your life. Not to mention, you will be desperately unhappy unless you are in a relationship.

Being single is a gift; one that must be understood to be appreciated. Embrace it, savor it, and respect that you need this time alone. Plus, time well-spent in single town will benefit your future relationships as well. Strong relationships stem from strong individuals.

So, choose to be single for now or forever. As long as you maintain a positive perspective about your choice, you will be happy.

After all, it will always be there for you. Welcoming you back with warmth and good company any time you need it, single town is far from deserted and always available.

Single is a Choice

The Perks to Being Single

Other than the obvious Netflix binge watching with an unholy amount of sweets that you must own up to no one, there are a million perks to being single.

This is the time to be selfish (not in a bad way), dedicated to finding and pleasing the true you. One hundred percent of your energy can now be invested into yourself, what you enjoy, and what you need. Use that powerful resurgence to jumpstart your new life.

In this book, we will discuss trying new things, making time for old things, and traveling to places you've always wanted to go. There is nothing and no one to hold you back, so embrace this wonderful time of self-discovery and life.

These can be small satisfactions (like taking a dance class, learning a new language, or trying a new restaurant), or it can be larger life choices (like moving to a new city or starting a new career). You can be the judge on what personal explorations are right for you.

There is such freedom and opportunity when you are single!

Take chances, try things, make mistakes, and enjoy yourself right now. **You** are the priority.

Perhaps you are a single parent, thinking that you simply don't have time for anything else. This book is for you too. Remember, you are a person, not just a parent. You must make time for yourself and discover yourself as much as any other member of single town.

The biggest perk to being single is the guilt-free opportunity to pamper and invest in yourself. Map out your goals, what you might eventually want in a mate, build your support system, and surround yourself with whatever makes you happy.

Right now, get out a pen and paper. Write down at least 10 things that you enjoy or want to try. Give your aspirations a voice. This is your opportunity to do anything and be anyone. You can re-create yourself completely if you want or you can just try a few new hobbies. It's up to you.

This is not a chapter of patience and sacrifice, rather a time for renewal. So, don't waste a minute of it!

6

Single, Not Alone

The Value of Friendships

"Good connections can improve health and increase longevity" (Harvard Health Publications, 2010).

Humans are meant to connect and socialize, it's in our nature. Unfortunately, many wrongly lump being single in with being alone—this is completely false.

In fact, single town is the ideal place to make new friends and foster the nurturing required for that friendship to grow into something meaningful.

You can enjoy friendships of many kinds, but the value of investing in a like-minded friend who either understands your current situation or is living a similar situation cannot be overstated. How can you find such a gem? You must seek them out!

Seek out friends

How to Meet Friends:

- Join a support group
- Join bible study or a church
- Talk to people at your gym
- Take a class
- Start a new hobby
- Join Meetup.com
- Ask people for friend suggestions
- Try an appropriate app for meeting friends
- Join a club or organization
- Talk to people at your work
- Volunteer

7

Many people choose to stay in unsatisfying romantic relationships simply because they fear being alone. They fear isolation. Rather than pursuing healthy friendships that bring out the best in themselves, helping them to grow and offering them support, they "settle" for a less than ideal romantic partner. Understand that you deserve better! Again, being single is a choice, and likewise, being in a relationship should be a choice as well. Friendships can fulfill your need for connection and closeness, so never settle.

Did you know that having a best friend at work makes you 7 times more likely to feel engaged in your job, according to researcher Tom Rath? And if your best friend is committed to a healthy diet, you are 5 times more likely to abide by a healthy diet yourself.

Well-chosen friendships garner personal successes beyond anything you could attain alone.

Once you have identified a worthwhile friendship, invest in it wholeheartedly. Go beyond the basic birthday and Christmas acknowledgments! Dr. Lisa Firestone recommends 5 ways to maintain lifelong friendships.

Dr. Firestone's Tips to a Lasting Friendship:

- Be honest
- Repair misattunements
- Make time and show appreciation
- Alter your expectations and don't make assumptions
- Choose compassion over cynicism

One true friendship is worth more than a million acquaintances. It may take time, but once you find that true friend, you will always have someone to call at 3 a.m. without having to apologize.

Remember, human connection, contact, and interaction is vital to your happiness. Get together with your friends frequently. Offer smiles, eye contact, hugs, and touch. You will benefit from this as much as your friends do. We could all do with less screen time and more face-to-face contact.

Thoughtfulness is a common trait among people who maintain lifelong friendships. Check in on your friends frequently, celebrate their accomplishments, offer them comfort during hard times, and respect their passions and interests. Your friends want to know that you are there for them as much as they are there for you. So, be reliable and don't be afraid to show affection.

A good friend is not one who always agrees with you and never sparks controversy. Expect that you will have disagreements, this is human nature. How you choose to handle these more challenging times is what will determine the longevity of the friendship. A graceful nature and being quick to forgive is an asset when it comes to maintaining a friendship, but never forget to stand up for yourself in a respectful manner either.

Your friends will appreciate you in the good times, but they will love you if you can handle the bad times too. After all, isn't that

9

what you look for in a friend? Someone who can see past your faults and forgive you when you're at your worst because they know that underneath all that there exists an amazing person; that's friendship.

Take a moment and consider what you would value in a friend. Do you possess those traits yourself? Be the type of friend you would value.

My gifts

basketball
math
science
other

How I can contribute

volunteer/coach basketball
tutor in math & science
motivational speeches
talk about your career

Single, Not Alone

Community Involvement

Being a citizen of single town offers endless opportunities for involvement. Not only is community involvement essential for your longevity, it's also a great way to make friends while benefitting others.

The simple act of serving others reminds us how lucky we are, how small many of our problems are by comparison, and how good it feels to improve the life of another human being. Community involvement gives your life deep purpose while weaving you intricately into your community's fabric. You truly can make a difference.

You offer unique skills, talents, and ideas, each contributable. Make a thoughtful list of your gifts and decide how you can contribute them to your community.

Perhaps you are a good singer, artist, or story teller. Maybe you possess a rare set of knowledge that you could impart. Perhaps you are a master at social media. All of these can be invaluable when put to good use and toward your community.

Typically, your contributions become amplified when they are combined with others' talents. It offers you the chance to make new friendships, learn new things, and put your gifts to good use where they will be deeply appreciated.

These are lasting contributions with meaning.

(1) Tutoring in math and science
(2)

Need some ideas for community involvement? Start with your church, local shelter, or city council. If you are crafty, consider donating knitted blankets or hats to hospitals, shelters, or new mothers. If you have an interesting career, volunteer to speak about it at local schools or your library.

Volunteer at a senior center to read, sing, or visit with folks. Offer help to your animal shelter to care for or find homes for animals. Attend community events. Volunteer at your library. Join Habitat for Humanity or Big Brothers, Big Sisters.

There are also paid positions that offer a great deal of value to the community as well. Being the conductor of a community band or being a member of city council are both excellent ways to share your talent, make money, and benefit your community. You don't have to volunteer in order to contribute in a positive way. Taking money for your beneficial services does not lessen your contribution.

These are just a few examples to get you started. Get involved any way you can and your life will be better for it. A satisfying life comes from connections, and community involvement is an ideal way to make meaningful connections.

Perhaps you are shy or feel your contributions will be too meager to matter? No act of kindness is too small. Even a simple smile can have a ripple effect throughout a community, uplifting each of your neighbors who in turn uplift their neighbors. It's true, you may not witness the benefits you provide, but trust that they are there.

Single, Not Alone

Family

Love them, hate them, and everything in-between. Family can be a rich source of satisfaction and occasionally drama too!

Family is forever.

Perhaps you have always been close with your family, or perhaps now that you are single you are ready to mend some broken or neglected relationships with kin. Remember, when it comes to family, there is never a bridge too burned—family is forever. Now is the perfect time to nurture those ties. In many ways, you ought to treat family relationships as you would lifelong friendships and follow the same principles.

If distance is an issue, set a weekly time to chat and catch up. If you are lucky enough to live close to family, reach out to them. Get together for an outing or a walk.

Surrounded by family may be where you feel most comfortable speaking your mind and being yourself, but don't hold a grudge if you receive some constructive criticism. It's natural. Embrace what you find useful and let go of whatever you don't. We don't choose our family the way we choose our friends, so the variety of personalities and opinions can come with a tendency for more confrontation. But with more viewpoints comes more knowledge of the world.

Family can also mean children of your own. Being a single parent brings many challenges and a great deal of joy (I know, I am a single mom of 3).

Sometimes, your greatest contribution to this world isn't something you do but rather it's someone you raise.

If you are a single primary caregiver, loneliness may not cross your mind in the traditional sense. If anything, it's solitude you seek! Take satisfaction and pride in your dedication to raising your kids; it's one of the toughest jobs in the world, but it's also the most rewarding.

Foster that special bond you have with your children. They give you plentiful opportunities to practice patience and become a better version of yourself. They are like tiny mirrors that reflect your personality traits, both good and bad, so consider what you want reflected in those little mirrors.

Allow yourself to take breaks when you are a single parent. No one expects you to be a machine and no one will benefit from it either. Consider the quality of the time you spend with your kids and not just the quantity. It's easy for the quality to slip when you are stressed or when you don't allow yourself a break. You are a parent, but you are a person too, and your happiness depends on you safeguarding that aspect of yourself.

Single parents should pay particular attention to the "Exploring You" sections of this book. Learn to define yourself in terms other than just as your child's parent. You have interests, explore them.

If you are a single parent who only has partial custody, enjoy every moment you can with your kids and free yourself of the guilt when you can't be with them. Instead, use that time away to better yourself as a person, making yourself the best life example for your children. Showing them that happiness is possible as a single is a valuable life lesson for them and for you.

Single, Not Alone

Pets

There will always be those days when you want nothing more than to shut out the world and be left to your thoughts. Even in single town, this is normal and healthy. On days when socializing is a burden, a loving pet will still be welcome.

There is a pet for every soul and need. Dogs are deeply loyal, cats require less day-to-day work, fish offer beauty and ambiance, and a chicken offers eggs for food.

Consider your current living situation, previous experience, and possible level of commitment when deciding on a pet. And if you're not sure, you can volunteer as a foster pet parent for your animal shelter and test the waters of being a pet owner without all the commitment.

Many people develop deep feelings of affection for their pet and bond with them in a unique and loving way. Pets are often seen as therapeutic. They offer a quiet friendship.

You can tell your pet anything, not be judged, and feel better that you confided in someone.

Nurturing a pet also gives you a sense of purpose. You feel loved and needed. This can be especially valuable if you live alone.

Sharing your joy for your pet can also be an excellent icebreaker when meeting new people. Dog parks and dog beaches are the best example, but there are also cat shows and horse shows too. Whatever the occasion, these are people who share your same affections and passion for a given animal.

Deep in the eyes of a well-loved animal lies a wise old soul only its owner can see.

I am the proud owner of a Bengal cat. From "not an animal person" to Bengal-obsessed seemed to happen overnight. There is an entire community to which I now belong because of my newfound passion. I view this as a bonus, but the real prize is my pet. It is wonderful to come home to a happy animal ready to greet me and give me his full attention.

You may surprise yourself, as I did, and be ready for a pet during this time in your life, even if you have never had one before.

Exploring You

Trying New Things

Whether you are a new resident of single town carving out your unattached identity or a seasoned single who is well-accustomed to the lifestyle, continually exploring yourself and trying new things ought to be a top priority.

Why? Because you will get to know yourself better and push yourself to grow by venturing into new territory. And while you're at it, you will meet many other interesting people doing the exact same thing.

The internet makes finding events simple. Begin with looking up events for your town and surrounding areas. There may be a wine room hosting astronomy lectures, a nature center hosting guided hikes, or a farmer's market downtown. These are typically events that don't require you to sign up, so the commitment level is low.

You don't have to go bungee jumping to be considered adventurous! Just step outside your box a little.

Do some research. What are the most popular events in your town? How about in your state? Are there athletic events you want to watch or participate in?

Exploring new things can lend itself to short-term or long-term goals as well. Perhaps there is a race or triathlon in your city you wish to try. This could inspire many sessions of running, swimming, and biking. Maybe you want to enter something in the county fair. This could inspire you to sign up for some art classes beforehand.

If you are ready to mark your calendar regularly or have a specific interest, peruse through some community classes. You may find learning to sew, learning a language, a group trip to Europe, or Tai chi. Your local YMCA and library will have a calendar of events as well.

However, trying new things can be as simple as eating at a different restaurant, experiencing new spices and flavors. Or, trying a different sport, attending a concert, or volunteering.

Travel typically tops the list when it comes to trying new things and exploring. It wraps adventure, new food, new locale, new language, and new people all into one! Be adventurous and dream big when considering locations. Where have you always wanted to go?

Don't be inhibited by a foreign language or the fear of traveling alone. You could always travel with a tour group if you prefer, where meals and destinations are all planned for you. You could also consider a cruise that is all-inclusive. This allows you to enjoy the travel experience without the stress of planning and researching.

All of these explorations expand your world and color it more vibrantly.

It is this expansion that is key to a satisfying life.

Imagine a man with only one hobby, golf. He eats, sleeps, and breathes golf. All of his conversations and spare time revolve around golf. Imagine his reaction if he suffered an injury and could no longer participate in his beloved hobby. His laser-focused world would be destroyed! Do not allow your world to be dependent on one single interest—explore. Expand your outlook and interests so your happiness is not dependent on one thing.

Exploring our world helps us explore ourselves too. You never know what you might end up enjoying or who you may meet in the process.

Exploring You

Reliving Old Enjoyments

Think back to your happiest childhood moments; the smells, tastes, and happenings. Reliving those happy moments can be deeply satisfying because they are at the core of who you are as a person.

I enjoy reliving toast dipped in hot chocolate, a favorite winter snack for me and my siblings. You may enjoy playing an instrument you used to practice, singing old songs, or catching up with old friends.

Take the best pieces from your past and incorporate them into your present to deepen your roots.

Especially when you are feeling shaky on your own identity, which can happen all too easily after a breakup, reliving old enjoyments can bring out confidence and self-understanding.

21

For some, old enjoyments were abandoned during the course of a relationship, and the neglect left a small hole in their identity. This is the time to recommit to those lost enjoyments.

You can reinvent or update your old enjoyments too. The point is to take that happy memory and sew it into your present reality however it may be practical. For example, if you grew up near lavender fields but now live in a city, you could fragrance your apartment with lavender soaps and candles or hang pictures of lavender fields. It's a constant reminder of a happy time, and we as humans need many reminders to be happy.

My grandmother had mint plants growing all around her house, where I used to play each summer growing up. As you can imagine, the smell of mint reminds me of that time and place. Drinking mint tea and smelling mint candles is my way of reinventing that old enjoyment and keeping it close to my heart.

Consider the sights and smells of your happiest memories. Which locations meant the most to you? Elements from your happiest moments ought to be incorporated into your present as much as possible, in whatever way possible. Relive your memories through your five senses to offer yourself ideas about how to reinvent them to fit with your present life.

Hold on to these defining elements voraciously, even when you are no longer a single. These are pieces of your identity.

It's the trees with the deepest roots that can withstand the strongest storms.

Exploring You

Hobbies, Interests, Involvements

  We singles are blessed with control over our personal time and how it's best spent. For every person, there is at least one hobby or interest that sparks great passion and satisfaction. If you haven't found yours yet or would like to expand your repertoire, consider some of these suggestions.

Learn a new instrument
Join a choir
Take a cooking class
Take a dance class
Coach a sport
Sign up for a race
Start a store on Zazzle
Write a book
Read a book
Adopt a pet
Garden
Knit or crochet
Learn a new sport
Travel
Join a meetup group
Host a dinner
Attend a community event
Run for city council
Start a club
Go camping
Become a mentor
Learn to draw or paint

Hobbies, Interests, Involvements

Take a massage class
Teach a community class
Join a group exercise class
Go horseback riding
Try a new restaurant
Start a collection
Learn archery
Attend a rodeo
Try a new video game
Try Pilates or yoga
Try meditation
Visit a touristy destination
Enter a competition
Start a blog
Become a wine or beer expert
Join a church group
Write a cookbook of family recipes
Make a photo calendar
Enter a poetry contest
Try to break a world record
Try to invent a new recipe
Invent an app
Learn photography
Attend a festival
Try paragliding
Volunteer at a farm
Start a booth at your farmer's market
Start a charity
Donate to a good cause
Join an astronomy club
Learn chess
Submit to an opinion column

Hobbies, Interests, Involvements

Play the lottery
Learn to brew beer
Learn candle making
Scuba dive
Map your genealogy
Journal
Invent something
Learn origami
Attend a renaissance faire
Take a self-defense class
Start a YouTube channel
Learn soap making
Become an extreme couponer
Volunteer
Grow your own herbs
Play the stock market
Join the PTA
Host a foreign exchange student

    Consider this list a jumping off point and brainstorm about what you've always wanted to try. Start with things you think you will enjoy the most before venturing into uncharted territory that may leave you less excited. But, you honestly never know what you'll enjoy until you try. You may surprise yourself.

    I tried parasailing and it was one of the worst experiences of my life, vomiting in mid-air over the ocean while on-looking tourists snapped photos to capture the memory. It soured me to trying new things for quite some time. I often think of how I should have started with something smaller, like going for a boat ride first. No doubt, that experience wouldn't have been as dramatic and I likely would have felt safer about trying more endeavors.

Years later, I picked up crochet and fell in love with the craft. It inspired me to take on more activities and stretch myself. I hosted a playgroup while living abroad in France, I started a blog, I adopted a Bengal cat, and I have done many other adventurous things since my parasailing disaster.

You can't let negative experiences keep you from discovering the world and living fully. And yes, you will have some negative experiences, hopefully not as embarrassing as mine or as public. You will learn to dust yourself off and try something new, just as I did. And I'm glad that I did!

Get creative and be open-minded. There are so many hobbies nowadays and so many ways in which to discover them.

Cures for Loneliness

Habits and Routines

Loneliness is part and parcel with the human condition. Anyone can suffer from loneliness, single or not.

Habits and routines are a simple solution for keeping loneliness at bay, because your brain experiences satisfaction when routines are executed as expected. They also help to pass time quickly and soothe anxiety.

My favorite routine is to have a cup of tea and read a good book before bed. Your routine may be a morning cup of coffee, attending church on Sunday, reading the newspaper, or listening to the radio at a certain time.

It matters very little what you do in your habit or routine, simply that you have certain rituals that act as anchors throughout your day. Eating lunch at noon each day is a routine, or driving to work the same way each day.

Invest in some healthy routines, like meditation or going for an evening walk. Your body and mind will come to expect it and you will reap rewards other than just avoiding loneliness.

When you feel yourself slipping into a lonely state—pushing the outside world away—have a go-to routine ready for soothing. Pick up a book with familiar characters, like Harry Potter, or watch a familiar TV show. Listening to a familiar radio show or song can also help.

If you are very new to single town and feeling the pangs of loss from broken routines, invest in making new routines for yourself. This is actually quite critical to your happiness as an individual and as a single.

New routines provide new connections and a sense of self as an individual.

Performing rituals you once enjoyed with a romantic partner will leave you feeling sad and dissatisfied. Disentangle yourself from these routines as much as possible and carve out new habits that you enjoy on your own. This will reinforce your happiness as a single.

Defining your routines defines your new life. Be conscious when selecting and creating routines, make them concise and calming. Make them pleasurable.

Cures for Loneliness
Goals and Contributions

Your life will be satisfying if you 1) feel like you've accomplished something and 2) feel like you matter.

Your goals can be big or small, creative or unoriginal. Think about your goals. Write down a list of at least 10 ideas and keep it in your sock drawer, so every now and again you can check on your progress. There is satisfaction in accomplishing something that's meaningful to you, but there is deeper satisfaction in accomplishing a specific goal you set for yourself and worked toward.

This is not a section for me to list goals from which you choose, because goals are personal. The only one who can make your list is you. What do you hope to accomplish in life and how can you get there? Can you break that down into attainable pieces? What sparks your passion? What do you value most? This is a time to delve into your core beliefs.

One of my goals was to raise my children in my small hometown in New Mexico. I want them to appreciate a simple life surrounded by nature and family. It took me a decade, but I am finally home, and the satisfaction is incredible.

Simply selecting your goals can help you define yourself and understand yourself better. Each of your goals is connected to your values. Take the time to ask yourself why you value it. Respect your goals and do all you can to accomplish them, as they are a deep part of you and how you view the world.

Contributions can be a type of goal or something altogether different. There may be a sudden opportunity for you to help someone in need that could not have been premeditated and planned like a goal. But the satisfaction gained from contributing is tremendous. You can contribute to a cause, person, or community, to name a few. Just keep your heart and mind open to opportunities and they will come to you.

In the end, what you feel you've accomplished and whom you've impacted will likely be the criteria on which you judge the value of your life.

You are the ultimate judge on whether you had a good life, a happy life. Visualize yourself far into the future, asking yourself whether you feel you mattered. Now, make sure that answer is "yes." Get involved and make a difference in this world in a way that only you can.

Cures for Loneliness

Happiness is a Mindset

Imagine two women, one rich and one poor, both given a single loaf of bread and a pitcher of water for the day. The rich woman is appalled at the meagerness of the offerings, while the poor woman is overjoyed by the bounty of her feast. The same situation, different mindsets, and different reactions.

It is not the situation that needs to change, only your mindset.

Happiness is a choice. One that you must choose day in and day out. Your life situation may never change, but your state of mind—being happy—certainly can.

It isn't easy to be happy, even though it may seem like it ought to be. But before you become frustrated by this human condition to desire more, consider the benefits of it. If people were always happy, they would not be motivated to make changes, push themselves, change the world, or work hard. From our dissatisfaction, we gain invention, motivation, and determination. There is purpose in our strife.

But this doesn't mean we have to accept unhappiness. Simply acknowledge that it is generally the default and there is a reason for that. Happiness is a choice you must make.

Yes, it's work to train your brain to be happy, but positivity gets easier with practice, because your brain strengthens those pathways as they are exercised more. At first, you may benefit from saturating your outside surroundings with positivity (peaceful music, motivational quotes, avoidance of negativity) until your internal environment is stronger in its state of happiness. Over time, your mind will prefer happiness.

Starting a gratitude journal is an excellent way to improve your mindset. Simply write down the things for which you are grateful in your life or for that day. You are drawing attention and awareness to the good that is in your life, the good that may have otherwise been overlooked. You may be grateful for your job, that your child slept all night, your health, an unusually short commute that day, or any number of things. There is so much good in your life but you have to pay attention in order to appreciate it. That's what the gratitude journal is for. You will learn to view your day differently, looking for things to record. You learn to seek out positivity.

Practice positive affirmations, reciting uplifting words to yourself daily to reinforce your happiness. Say things like, "I am confident. I am happy. I can make the world a better place." Any affirmation will benefit your mindset. These may not be things you believe wholeheartedly, yet, but over time they will help you focus on the things you want. Think of it like exercise, that is, unless you really dislike exercise! In that case, think of chocolate. That always makes me happy!

Healthy Mind and Body

Diet and Exercise

The mind and body are one, woven together and reliant on one another.

     Nurturing one will benefit the other, and likewise, neglecting one will bring demise to the other.

     I am no advocate of the lemon and cayenne pepper liquid diet, nor am I a fan of any diet at all. Chocolate is high on my list of priorities, as stated previously! But I do insist on eating balanced meals and snacks filled with foods close to their truest form in nature. I also exercise at least 4 times a week. My dedication goes far beyond vanity. I do it for my sanity and life satisfaction.

In our modern times of plentiful food and desk jobs, obesity is quickly becoming a way of life. And in single town, eating out is more common than home cooking. The result is an unhealthy body that inevitably diseases the mind.

It is easy to understand why practicing an unhealthy diet is so pervasive, with desk jobs being the norm and work weeks plus commutes taking up most of our daily hours. There is little time or energy left to focus on diet and exercise. But the real issue is lack of priority.

We don't prioritize our diet or our need for exercise. But these are the two biggest cures and preventions of disease. They ought to be high on our priority lists!

Take control of your health and happiness! Without depriving yourself of the things you love, start to make healthy dietary changes. Eat more greens, whole fruits, start cooking, or try hard-boiled eggs. Slowly, your palette will adjust and your body will feel more energetic. Add in some exercise, like 30 minutes of walking a day or light weight lifting 3 times a week. Your brain will be spoiled with delicious endorphins that offer happiness.

You may be surprised what a difference small changes can make.

But who can you really trust in this world when it comes to honest advice about diet and exercise? Trust a nutritionist, dietitian, or your doctor. Ignore fads and never pay money for pills or shakes. Good old-fashioned healthy eating and moderate exercise is all you need. I am a particular fan of body weight exercises, as they require no equipment, are gentle on the body, and can be executed anywhere easily. You don't even need to pay for a gym membership to be healthy!

If you have never exercised or haven't in quite some time, you may need to get a physical and check in with your doctor first.

Pay attention to your blood pressure results before launching into a new cardio routine.

Only commit to what you can deliver consistently because it is the consistency that will offer results. Going hard for two days will net few benefits, but adding in a simple 15-minute walk every morning for a month will provide benefits you can see and feel.

Allow yourself to build on these successes and bask in the happiness they offer.

Perspective is key when it comes to diet and exercise, just as it was for feeling that your single status is your choice. These delicate topics must be approached with positivity and from a place of self-love. If your mind is not on board, your body will certainly ignore your efforts!

If there is one motto to live by in the category of diet or weight loss let it be "make your food choices based on what your body needs to flourish, because you want what's best for it; it deserves the finest nutrients."

Fueling your body with healthy foods allows your mind to function at full capacity, without fog or fatigue. Our modern foodstuffs—engineered and prepackaged meals—can't offer the type of nutrition your body deserves. Spoil yourself with real food grown from the earth and with little to no manipulation or processing.

Avoid falling into the mind trap that this way of eating is some type of punishment. That's negativity and ignorance that you don't need, bringing undeniable depression to the short-sighted thinker. Just try eating healthy foods and see how you feel. Of course, keep balance in mind too! Not every choice has to be healthy, you can have your cake and eat it too. I aim for 80% of my choices to be healthy and 20% to be otherwise.

This methodology has worked well for me for years. After three babies, I am still healthy and without excess weight. I have a deep appreciation for the benefits of diet and exercise, and I am consistent in my commitment. <u>I attribute my success to my mindset.</u> I love my body, I want the best for it, so I feed it well.

It's true that I'm a scientist and a personal trainer. I have more knowledge than the average Joe when it comes to the topics of diet and exercise, but you needn't a degree in order to make positive changes in your life. All you need is determination.

Don't worry about your weight, a number on a scale. Spend less time in front of a mirror, determining whether you look good or not. What matters is how you feel. Does your body feel good today? What can you do to help your body feel good today? Focus on this and everything else will fall into place. You will feel happy AND you will look good.

True beauty is a feeling, not a feature.

Healthy Mind and Body
Meditation and Massage

Residents of single town sometimes experience less physical touch than those in romantic partnerships. Touch is so essential to a human body and mind, this needs to be supplemented, and massage is the perfect supplement. Think of it as medicinal.

Diet and exercise are the foundation for a healthy mind and body, but massage and meditation are the vitamins and medicine.

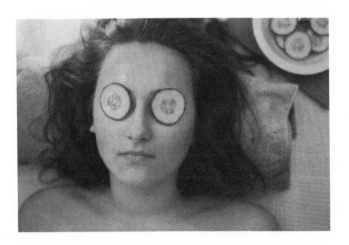

If you have the money to invest in professional massage or a meditation class, go for it! If not, consider free methods that are just as affective. Self-myofascial release is a technique for self-massage with incredible benefits. Foam rollers, lacrosse balls, and even tennis balls are tools used to press against your muscles, causing them to release and relax. Along with the tension, waste-filled fluids are released and your body rids them from your system.

Before starting self-myofascial release, ask a qualified practitioner or at least invest in a good book on the topic. There is a bit to know about the technique so that you don't injure yourself and cause more harm than good. There are a few categories of people who should not practice self-myofascial release or who should proceed with caution, such as pregnant women and those with arthritis. But, for most of the population, it is a simple and extremely beneficial technique for your mind and body.

It doesn't require fancy equipment either. You can search Amazon for self-myofascial release or foam roller, but you can use an old tennis ball if you have one. There are many products for trigger point and self-myofascial release. If you have the money to test them out, go for it, otherwise, just use what you have. The type of equipment is far less important than the commitment to practice and the consistency. You can get excellent results from practicing self-myofascial release once a week.

What areas should you target with this method? If you have a desk job, like most people do, aim for releasing your hips, between your shoulders, and your neck at the base of your head. These areas become extra tight and hold a great deal of stress and toxic fluids. Apart from these main areas, the soles of your feet are incredibly important to release.

Sue Hitzmann, the inventor of the MELT method, is a great resource for gaining knowledge about self-myofascial release and self-massage. Some of her resources are listed at the end of this book.

Your body is the tool by which you experience life. Maintain it well.

Meditation is less physical than massage but no less important. Backed by stacks of research studies, meditation offers proven health benefits for the mind and body. It may seem simple to sit quietly and focus on breathing, but this practice may prove to be a challenge! In creep your thoughts, emotions, repressed memories, and all the other things you have tried to mentally avoid. Meditation is an exercise in controlling your mind, accepting your thoughts. Start slowly and be patient with yourself. Success will come with time and it will be well-worth your efforts. There is no substitute to finding your own peace within.

Being a member of single town allows you to become more self-reliant. You must learn to trust yourself, your mind, your thoughts, and your inner calm. Meditation is the route to all of this.

You can use an app, CD, or instructor to guide you through meditation practice if you are unsure about how to begin. Guided meditation is the simplest place to start. But all you really need is a quiet space.

To begin meditation, sit or rest in a relaxed position in a safe space. Your environment should be calm and peaceful. Close your eyes and allow yourself to focus on the moment, the environment, the present. Breathe deeply and allow thoughts to come and go.

Do not be fooled into thinking meditation is easy or pleasant at first. In fact, it may feel like mental vomit. That isn't a beautiful description but it is appropriate! Allow this to bubble up, calm it, control it, and wipe it away. This takes practice.

It took me many months of serious meditative practice to break through my vomit-thought plateau. It happened suddenly too, an instantaneous calm. It was my first experience reaching my inner peace. Although it only lasted a moment, I never forgot the feeling. You won't either, once you get there.

Over time, your mental strength will grow and your thoughts will become calmer and less frequent while meditating. The result is having stronger inner peace that you feel even when you aren't meditating. This is the core of a satisfying life.

Healthy Mind and Body
List of Calming Techniques

When your body and mind are anxious, stressed, or over-taxed in some way, calming techniques come in handy to bring you back to neutral. We've discussed exercise, meditation, and massage. Apart from those essential calming techniques, here are a few others.

Take a warm bath

Smell lavender

Go for a walk in nature

Practice deep breathing

Look at the clouds

Rest your head between your knees

Imagine a beautiful nature scene

Count back from 100

Drink a cup of warm tea

Call a friend

Write in a journal

Find a distraction

41

List of Calming Techniques

Read your favorite book

Pet an animal

Cuddle with a fuzzy blanket

Sit by a fire

Light your favorite candle

Pray

Draw, paint, or color

Listen to calming music

Garden

Clean

Organize your closet

Practice mindfulness

Stretch

Step outside and change surroundings

Listen to ocean sounds or nature sounds

Take a nap

Cry

Rock in a rocking chair

Play an instrument

Use guided imagery

List of Calming Techniques

Take a hot shower

Go for a drive

Hold a pillow to your tummy

Eat some chocolate

Try aromatherapy

Practice containment exercises

Describe your present moment with each of your 5 senses

Rub your temples, hands, and feet

Think of a time when you were happy

Perform an act of kindness

Sit on a park bench

Watch the sunset

Look at the stars

Practice reflexology

Hold a comforting object

Smell eucalyptus

Go for a run

Remember, your brain can be trained. This can be good or bad depending on what you allow. The more you allow yourself to be in a state of anxiety, depression, or dissatisfaction, the more you will default there. Use these calming techniques to bring you back to neutral and from there, work toward happiness as your new default mindset.

I find nature to be the most universal calming technique. It can be simply taking a break from your computer to look out the window or as impactful as visiting the Grand Canyon. Being in nature, looking at pictures of nature, listening to nature sounds, and mentally imagining nature is healing and helps us find perspective in our world. It lowers our stress hormones and improves our thinking ability. There is plentiful research around the topic, with the frontrunners taking place in Japan and Korea.

I am lucky to live in an area with plentiful nature and hiking trails. Not a day passes where I don't get outside and enjoy the mountains and trees. However, you may not have that ability if you live in a city. Instead, invest in houseplants and take time to look at pictures of nature. National Geographic is an excellent source for that.

For more on calming techniques, look for my second book in this series, "1000 Ways to De-Stress, Relax, and Self-Soothe." In-depth details are given on how to calm your emotions—anger, anxiety, depression, and stress. You will learn techniques to calm as well as methods for accepting relaxation. You can enjoy an exclusive excerpt at the end of this book.

Calming takes practice, it's a skill. It is not as simple as it may seem and it requires effort and investment on your part.

Healthy Mind and Body

Benefits of Therapy

Remember when we talked about the road that led you to single town? There may be things along your road that require a professional help for healing. Otherwise, you may find yourself on a roundabout, circling that spot over and over, unable to get past it.

There are many therapists and many therapy techniques, so don't be quick to count all of them out. You may need to try a few before you find something that works for you.

If you suffer from anxiety, depression, or PTSD, therapy may seem obvious. However, most people can benefit from therapy in some capacity. Perhaps you have anger management issues, are overly critical of others, suffer from perfectionism, or lack motivation.

Therapy is an opportunity for self-improvement.

None of us are perfect, nor should we try to be, but improving ourselves allows us to improve our relationships and outlook on life, making happiness and satisfaction more attainable.

Therapy offers a less biased viewpoint. Your family and friends are great for comfort and reassurance, but when it comes to self-improvement and receiving constructive criticism well, therapy is likely a better option. You know you are there to improve yourself. You trust this person has no ulterior motives.

Keep in mind, therapy is a relationship. You are forming a bond with your therapist so that you can open up completely (thorns and all) in order to analyze issues and work on them appropriately. You may not bond with just anyone, and that's okay. Be picky when it comes to choosing a therapist and don't be afraid to "break up" with your therapist either. This is all for your benefit, so make it positive.

If you have more serious biological issues, such as depression or anxiety, your therapist can help you determine whether medication is the right option. For some people, medication like SSRIs are invaluable because their genetically determined physiology just can't manufacture what is needed to overcome these disorders otherwise. You should not pass judgment on yourself or others when medication is used. We are all different, our bodies are different, our physiological needs are different, and we should all respect that.

Determining which medication suits you best can take time and patience as well. There can be side effects that may make you question your decision. Keep an open mind and open communication with your doctor. Most of these side effects only last a few weeks while your body adjusts. Do your best to listen to your body but also practice patience. Never just stop taking medications! That can be even harder on your body and it can have very negative results. You should always wean slowly, both on and off these medications.

Many people take medication for PTSD, anxiety, OCD, and depression. These are very common diagnoses with commonly prescribed medications that have been monitored for years. You can feel comfortable taking them for a short period or for life. Some people need these medications due to their biology. It can make all the difference to them and significantly improve their life. You may benefit from medication and you may not. Talk to your doctor and listen to your body. Only you can decide what's right.

There are many natural approaches as well, and some of these may work beautifully for you. Soothing techniques and the calming methods listed previously certainly fall into this category. Diet and exercise are the best natural approaches.

Beware of unregulated herbs and herbal remedies, however. These are not tested and monitored the way medications are regulated. It can be easy to overdose or to ingest something that was not manufactured well, leading to toxicity and complications. Understand that many medications are derived from herbs and there is precedent for their use. The issue is with the dosing and manufacturing, not with the credibility of the herb itself.

Both Ayurvedic and Chinese medicine traditions have been practiced far longer than any type of Western medicine, and both employ herbs as a type of natural remedy. In the hands of a trained professional, the use of natural remedies and herbs can be effective and safe. Take your time to find a top-rated practitioner if you choose to go this route. They should be licensed.

We all strive for the same goal: to be happy. And we all have the opportunity to meet that goal, regardless of our road, regardless of our previous choices. We can choose to be happy.

You can choose to be happy. There is no challenge here on earth that cannot be overcome in order to achieve happiness and satisfaction in life.

Some members of single town have suffered divorce, death of a spouse, or other traumatic events. These trials have offered personal growth and a well-defined road that ought to be appreciated and accepted, but left behind nonetheless.

It is time to get out there. Make friends, try new things, savor moments and people, because these are the elements of life. You are a valuable member of single town and society with much to contribute and enjoy.

You are given one life, one opportunity here on earth. In the span of the universe, it will be nothing but a blink. Don't waste a single minute.

Extra Resources

Beyond this book, there are many resources I recommend that can aide you in your quest to finding happiness alone. These are books I happen to find interesting and engaging, perhaps you will as well, but perhaps you won't. We are all different. Allow these suggestions to be a starting point for you. Gather more information on your interests, establish new routines, and be an individual worth knowing. Fill your life with passion and happiness.

Please note, I have no affiliation with any of these products nor do I receive compensation for mentioning them. Consider the category and concept more than the exact product mentioned.

Books Available on Amazon:

"The Complete Book of Essential Oils and Aromatherapy, Revised and Expanded" by Valerie Ann Worwood.

"The Reflexology Atlas" by Bernard C. Kolster.

"Positive Thought Cards" by Louise Hay.

"Destinations of a Lifetime: 225 of the World's Most Amazing Places" by National Geographic.

"Gifts Differing: Understanding Personality Type" by Isabel Briggs Myers.

"Real Happiness: The Power of Meditation: A 28-Day Program" by Sharon Salzberg.

"How to Stop Worrying and Start Living" by Dale Carnegie.

"The Mindful Way Through Depression" by Mark Williams.

"The Big Book of Hobby Ideas" by D.J. Gelner.

"Trigger Point Therapy Workbook" by Clair Davies.

"Herbal Recipes for Vibrant Health" by Rosemary Gladstar.

"The MELT Method: A Breakthrough Self-Treatment System" by Sue Hitzmann.

"Mediterranean Diet for Beginners: The Complete Guide" by Rockridge Press.

"The Power of Affirmations - 1,000 Positive Affirmations (Law of Attraction in Action)" by Louise Stapely.

"The Daily Book of Positive Quotations" by Linda Picone.

Products Available on Amazon:

MELT Hand & Foot Treatment Kit (for self-massage)

MELT Soft Body Roller (for self-massage)

Brookethorne Naturals Relax Therapeutic
Body Massage Oil, Lavender, Peppermint and
Marjoram (for self-massage)

Aromatherapy Top Essential Oils Set 100%
Pure & Therapeutic Grade - Basic Sampler
Gift Set & Kit (for calming)

Traditional Medicinals Organic Chamomile Tea
(for calming)

Adult Coloring Book Designs: Stress Relief
Coloring Book: Garden Designs, Mandalas,
Animals, and Paisley Patterns (for calming)

The Happiness Project One-Sentence Journal:
A Five-Year Record (for happiness)

Questions that Lead to Happiness

       Take some time to answer each of these questions honestly. These answers are at the core of finding happiness and maintaining it in your life. Over time, your answers may change. This is normal because you will grow and learn as you move through life. If an answer doesn't come to you readily, make a note and come back to it. This may be an area on which to spend extra thought.

1) What are my benefits to being single?
2) Have I accepted my road that led me here?
3) What traits do I value in a friend?
4) How can I be a good friend?
5) Am I close with my family?
6) Are there relationships I should mend?
7) Would I adopt a pet?
8) What are my interests and hobbies?
9) What would I like to explore or try?
10) What are my core beliefs?
11) What are my short-term goals?
12) What are my life goals?
13) What are my happiest memories?

14) How can I reinvest in my old interests?
15) What calms and soothes me?
16) How much time do I spend in nature?
17) What new routines have I created since becoming single?
18) How would I like to contribute to my community?
19) What type of exercise would I enjoy?
20) What healthy foods do I enjoy?
21) Do I accept my body?
22) How can I make my body feel good?
23) How do I care for my body?
24) What positive affirmations can I recite?
25) What negative thoughts do I repeat?
26) How can I break the cycle of negative thoughts?
27) Would I try yoga or meditation?
28) Would I consider therapy?
29) When would medication be appropriate?
30) Would I prefer natural remedies?
31) Do I feel happy?

About the Author

Katharine Benelli Coggeshall is a scientist, personal trainer, independent author, and mother of 3. Living in the mountains of New Mexico, she enjoys hiking and playing with her kids in nature. She is also passionate about chocolate and her Bengal cat. Katharine has been published by Blue Mountain Arts, Adelaide Literary Magazine, and Inklings Publishing Group. She enjoys writing non-fiction, especially self help, as well as poetry.

If you enjoyed this book, please review it on Amazon and GoodReads! Reviews are the best way to support an author.

Connect with Katharine on her author pages on Amazon and Goodreads to stay up-to-date on recent publishings and blog posts.

More Titles by Katharine:

"101 Reasons I'd Rather Marry My Cat"

A humorous book from a female's perspective that is sure to bring a smile to your face.

"The Wedding Vows Chapbook"

Sample and inspirational wedding vows to help you write your own verse.

"Baby Boomers Guide to Retirement"

A guide covering a wide variety of retirement topics, not just finances.

Coming Soon:

"1000 Ways to De-Stress, Relax, and Self-Soothe"

Part 2 of the single's guide and self-help series.

Exclusive excerpt:

Calm Anger

Embrace this primal emotion, for it represents passion in your life. Where anger strikes and devastation reigns, you are marking the people, places, and things that mean the most to you in this world. Anger is closely correlated with love—consuming, fiery, and passionate. Of course, it does not FEEL like love. In fact, hate is used more frequently to describe one's reason for eruption. But do not be quick to dismiss this theory of correlation.

Consider a time when you were enraged and ask yourself why you felt that way. Were your values or beliefs being challenged in some way? Did you fear you would lose something or someone you hold dear? The greater your passion, the greater your anger.

This is not something to be changed; passionate people contribute enormously to our world. Squelching out your passion would strip away your identity, so both emotions—love and anger— must remain.

Here, you will learn to calm your anger once it has been ignited. Allow yourself to feel it, if only for a moment, before taming it. These are techniques to calm, not suppress or avoid, your anger. Some may work for you, others may not. We are all different.

Made in the USA
Columbia, SC
26 February 2018